Itch

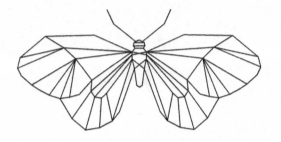

Nicki Heinen
Itch

Lorgnette Series

First published in 2017
by Eyewear Publishing Ltd
Suite 333, 19-21 Crawford Street
Marylebone, London W1H 1PJ
United Kingdom

Typeset with graphic design by Edwin Smet
Printed in England by Lightning Source

ISBN 978-1-911335-58-0

Eyewear wishes to thank Jonathan Wonham for his generous patronage of our press.

WWW.EYEWEARPUBLISHING.COM

For Mum

and in loving memory of G&G

How hard it is to say what that wood was,
a wilderness, savage, brute, harsh and wild.
Only to think of it renews my fear!
So bitter, that thought, that death is hardly worse

Dante

'Anything's possible in Human Nature,'
Chacko said in his Reading Aloud voice...
'Love. Madness. Hope. Infinite joy.'

Arundhati Roy

TABLE OF CONTENTS

ITCH

There's a little thing of black
flicks from glass eye to mouth to heart –
fills me up.

No-one knows
how small my eye shrinks,
doctor can't help me.

Hearing radio noise
I shut my glass eye tight,
lock it out.

Night mouse
behind the sink
makes a scratch –
I itch it free.

Milk spills out of a cup

the leaves and the moon and the fence
reflect hush

I break codes with wallpaper.

What end
to the night watch in this asylum
on this night and again on the next?

THE ABANDONED

I imagine you in a glass box,
which I have kept secret and hidden.
It is rectangular and sits in the living room like a blood stain.
I polish it nightly, spraying with the brand that you prefer,
taking the kitchen towel in folds and smoothing the drops till its sides shine.
You look restful and safe.
While I sleep, you reach out and stroke my cheek.
It is better this, than to see the box empty,
my hands turning feathery with over-use and my hair growing greyer
in the mirror. The mirror shows me your shadow, soft as felt,
but when I ask it for a kiss it wisps away, a tower of ash dissolving in the breeze.
I ask my lovers if they will say my name, gently, as you did;
they cannot. They take the mirror and hold it up to my face.
'Look,' they say, 'you are alone.'

SELF

Nothing hurts like a dead moth

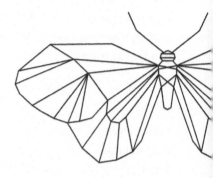

LEBOWSKI

I

He lifts a paw and taps me on the knee again and again, snagging on my
tights with clipped claws. Scoop him up, he fits in the crook of my elbow
like cold butter slowly melting. He smells of singed static, hot and needed
as baby wipes, antiseptic, lithium. I watch him run along the garden wall,
back legs white splash, his nose to wind. A knot in my heart, black fur
bondage as real as oil. My love is cat-shaped, he is mine.

II

Ecstasy, he makes – his noises. *Brroo-pip, rroaow, yeeaow, mii.* The purring
deep in his ruffle chest, against my body warm as a photocopier:
hrrrrrrrrrrrrrrrrrrrrrrrrrr. And suddenly: *Woo-hi-hi-haow,* a message from outer
space. His sneezes my love sonnets. *Hoorrrrrrhoorrrrrrr* all night again, my
divine mix-tape. *Crunch, crunch, slurp;* the food I provide not nearly the sum
of the love he gives.

III

When he miaows my ribs contract and I feel his little breath in my belly.
When I watch him eat I want to cry it's so beautiful. He is my animal
– more – my creature come to comfort me, my confidant, my endless
boundless fur-bound love, my sun-streaked white paw family. His small
claws hook around my hand when I stroke his pale stomach in bed and
I am complete. We are two animals sleeping, he and I, our breathing
regular, the end of his tail a feather in my mouth.

IV

This cat, he is not a regular cat. He is eyes wide as sherbet flying saucers, black glass fur. The highlights around his pink nose, on his throat, and underneath his lean frame – lightning white. Ears, antennae for dubious sound, pricked up like an olive pierced on a stick and put to mouth. I cannot tell how well this cat knows me. I cannot say how he is of the earth and of the sky, studded cloud in his paw and hailstorm in his pattering legs. His tail is sometimes curled under his body for safekeeping, like a pearl earring in a trinket box.

EUROPA

Tricksy Jupiter had a grin in his eye.

Spanning fields in a wink and wiping the god from his handsome brow
he landed four limbed,
hands to hooves and feet cloven
to the whisper of her summer dress.

His skin bred soft silk poils
as he gamboled among clean stiff poppies.

His back twisted on the ground,
and she in the noon light
caught his gaze just as blood clots in the vein.

Was it girl or plaything of dark skies came forward
long hand outstretched and lips flushed,
to the rise and trembling fall of his breaths?

She listened as the heat sighed her name
and the bend of her waist met his.

A swallow circled in the haze
where they lay,
her lashes dusting his pale coat,
her heavy lids closing.

The light shrank.

At evening,
cold air and ocean spray woke her.
Alone, her eyes drank in sea,
black waves rolling to the black horizon.

Sometimes, by night,
you can taste her salt tears in the waters.

FIRE-EATING IN WATERLOO

And in the damp spot beneath the stairs I placed the roses.
They burn yellow, gold, sunset pink,
the edges of each flower crumpling like broken skin.
It's a shame you'll never smell them.

The taste of oysters is sea glue, melted crayon, hair gel, semen,
the grit in each an aborted pearl. Whitstable, Chatressac, Loch Fyne.
A pearl on each earlobe, ripped tights, black bomber boots, I wait for my limo
on a thundery night in Clapton. Whisky in my left hand, a cigarette in the other.

Damp logs burn, hiss, offer up a priceless stink,
newspaper huffs and spits, fire moves like molten glass,
the proofs of my ten year novel are gone in two minutes and forty-three seconds,
I count. I feel a year younger with every page destroyed.

This is not an exercise in living, this is organ donation –
Feel the anguish and pronounce it dead.

SECRET

It's a bud picked off the tree,
a scab disfiguring,
a toe bleeding from high heeled shoes,
an old vegetable in the fridge
seeping.
It is mine and
I hate it
even more than I hate
lying in bed at night with sore eyes,
not sleeping.

INFERNO

The hospital I live in is a corrupt palace
as bloody as a monthly jab.
I can't speak for laughing,
stretched spasm
takes me to the lip of the canyon.
I look down on a house of cards,
dying inside but laughing laughing
till the beat in my chest snaps
and my head rocks.

I hear sirens and birdsong, they sound like signals from outer space.
I start dancing to pop, dancing with Chrissie who is dark and frightening.
Her hair is short, she bellows at me shuffling out of time.
I sit on the exercise bike in men's pyjamas with nothing underneath,
worried the flies will fall open and Nurse Allah-cum-Salaam will see.
I have no idea who I am and the rain beats so that the glass shakes.

Lock-up, lock-in, lock-tight.
I never knew freedom till it was gone,
never tasted liberty till
I was given 20 minutes a day.
Never understood why air is so fresh till I had only a courtyard for it.
Hysterics, broken glass, psychosis.

I refuse to eat slop,
smash the vending machine for crisps.
Nasty Nurse is not happy with me
for my repeated re-questionings:
'Are you the Devil? Am I in Hell?'
The bathroom smells of shit,
there's some smeared on the bath rail.

Greasy hair in braids,
I am starting to smell
of this institution.

A Coke can is my ash tray.
Locked in my room all night
and all day.
Puff puff
I'm not hurt,
though I bang on the door till my fist is red.

I stop eating anything but cheese sandwiches,
tell my psychiatrist everything tastes of piss.
He says this is an unusual symptom.
From the high windows flanking the long corridor
I can see a chimney pumping smoke from the distance.
Bodies are burnt there, this is a camp.
Turkish delight on my tongue
sticks like glue.
When the rain stops it's midnight and the lights are out.
But the chimney's still smoking.

The nurse says nothing as
he follows me, keeping the length of two corpses
behind me. I see him only out of the corner
of my eye. He comes in to my room
pushes the door behind him, it shuts
with a papery click

Shhh
he says, putting a finger to his lips. He is not much taller
than me, greasy, with a slipped face and stubble.
He puts a hand on each of my arms
steadies me in case I run
and leans in, smelling of hand sanitiser. Kisses me
long and hard, making sure I kiss back.
He moves his hands to my breasts and feels around slowly.
Then he leaves, closing the thin door.

I peel off my gold top and throw it in the bin,
sit in my bra for a minute. Then I put on a sweatshirt
and retch over the sink
wipe my mouth clean of smeared lipstick
with the blue and white NHS towel, and push open the door.
Walk to the office round the corridor
but he's got there first.

He is talking to a female nurse. She is round
with a silver brooch on her cardigan. Her hair is peppery grey and wispy

I take her out of the room
and tell her what has happened. He is inside typing
a report about me on the desktop computer. I can see my name at the top.

She puts on a sympathy face; the corners of her mouth turn down.
I hear her say
Nicki, dear, you're not well.
Nobody here would harm you.
Why don't you go to your room and have a little lie down.

LACE

The shop is closeted within a 1960s tower block and up three flights of concrete; we pass through an architect's office to get to it, iMacs and cardboard models ablaze with the light which slashes through the windows.

There are sixty white dresses on racks, a cabinet full of flowered head-dresses and then the veils — everything in this shop hanging stiffly like pelts, like trophies. The dresses delicate as origami, ridden with studded pearls and flowers and flickering gems. Who knew that there were this many shades of white?

My head is heavy with last night's wine and I feel as though I'm stepping into another life, one that could have been mine, one that should have been mine, one that is not mine.

She picks five, and the assistant reaches up to close the dark velvet curtain, blocking the bride from view as the secret ritual plays out. I sit on the patterned chaise longue, not knowing what I should be feeling, not knowing if I will ever be able to feel again.

I keep sitting, waiting; a drowning fly in a cup of milk. I feel nauseous; I still hurt here in the chest
here where he belonged, here where I could tap with ringed finger less than a year ago. A little year ago?
She comes out in her favourite and looks like rose drop on the tongue, lace covering her body in a tattoo of dust
The neck gathered with a delicate ruching so that her head emerges a golden phoenix, a whispering   victor, an ending note.
I look at her whiteness and breathe in, out, blinded by the texture of silken spun roses on the hips,
I want to dive into her and pull my own lost love from deep inside her, pull in and get my own dress   out.

23

MARRAKESH

The desert is dry as skin
the ground is
crisp nut brown
sometimes reddish blood

I run a fingernail to trace a line
it snags on the sun

blanched bushes punctuate the horizon
my eyes are filmy with looking

you have a red mouth
which spits seeds
they grow in the desert

your hot breath blooms

toes grow lichen and moss
a garden in gold
at night you snake into something
sinful and bold

you chase giants till they fall down dead
you pierce the shell of an egg
bleed it by blowing till it's hollow
blow till it daren't crack
you run and run
until the sun drowns in the sand
turning cold

RABBIT FUR STOLE

It hangs around my neck
a constant question

black fur gleams
hot and hairy
catches me by the throat
with a soft strangling

snowflakes fall
and latch on a hair
day and night merging

THE POLITICS OF THE UNDERWORLD WILL DESTROY US ALL

Trickle into THIS, you rump steak well cooked:
We are not expendable casino tokens,
we are not offal, mixed into nugget paste,
we are not invisible
and we are not taking it
any longer.
Make your choice,
or this world will crumble into thin and melting ice,
and you will drown along with us all –
as your hands sink below the bloody water,
we can still smell the shit on your fingers.

HELL'S ANGELS

A gun is a gun is a gun.

Melt gold and silver till the damn thing is gone.

PINK

I take it,
feel it surge and stretch
under the tongue
taste salted caramel,
suck the poison out
of the flower,
texture like ridged rice paper,
like warmed ice cream.
It grows and grows
till taste spills
and swills out
of my pink mouth.

THE FASHIONISTA MOTHS OF HIGHGATE

Black-eared, white winged, they edge in silently
frequencies unheard, they signal
each to each a whisper like whipped cream
each to each desirous of cloth, each to each nattily naked.

Silk slips, a luncheon of kings.
Cashmere, a royal buffet.

Polyester cardigan untouched.

Come to me, you Highgate moths,
and I will cover myself in velvet –
wings fluttering like cassette tape in the wind,
your tiny antennae pricking towards the virgin wool,
smother me in cotton and leave me blind as a blank book.

You come to destroy and
I can understand that.

THE PIANIST

He hears mouse scratch, clear bell,
static.
He hears insect steps and teddy bear
moans,
the deafened chimes and purring
under the covers.
He hears giggling and sobbing and
suppressed cries.
He hears you and me and all our
quieting. Bubbling water.
He hears the whisky secrets of them
all.
And out of it, he makes music.

SNOWSTORM

There is light breaking out from the queen's tomb
in a far forgotten city where the cars' jaws eat bread crusts
fed by urchins in velvet suits.
A gone land, sore threaded carpets made by moths on the palace floors,
a debt-ridden hungry place of hurricanes that pass by
devolved of power. *Click-clack* go the heels of the lawyers coming
to unseat the throne, *click-clack* go the elevator doors.
Leopards roam the streets, purring at the smell of gasoline.
Words whirl in storms, they are flown like kites by the urchin
velvet-suited children. The words are full of meaning; the children cheer.
Click-clack go the pistols of the police, coming to keep the poor hungry.
But there is light breaking out from the queen's tomb. You wander here,
and when I shake the globe, your pinched face fights against the waft of snow.

THE CROWS AT CHATRESSAC

You are sunk black.
Black scratches,
Thin bones feathered unkindly.

You eat light,
Fly into it with revulsion.

You make a noise like time travel,
Nibble at rebels for breakfast.

This is a bleak picture,
Coarse pepper scattered across the sky.

Soot speckled peach.
Ants on a blushing cheek.

Quick as feet
Sharp as flint.

Lifting like a Times Square elevator
Into a bony wind.
Caw, caw
With black beak
Which picks at scraps of ligament hungrily
Leaving mess.

If you turn on me I will hide and my shadow will tussle with you.
When you fly in clusters
Out of the tree by my window on a cold October morning,
I'll try not to throw plum stones at you.

JOURNEYING NORTH

Along the highway stand vats the size of giants' boots
electric pylons reaching for the moon
bats flitting homewards

we drive quietly and I think –
a grey dusk is as bad as sleepless dawn

the day a river of sighs
the night cold

and the text ticks on in the mind
'in the end there
will be no beginnings'

ACKNOWLEDGEMENTS

Some of these poems have been published in various online and print magazines and anthologies, thanks go to the editors of those: Magma, The Oxford Magazine (with special thanks to Bernard O'Donoghue), The May Anthologies, Rising Magazine, Holdfast Anthology, Blue of Noon Magazine, Shooter Literary Magazine, and Goldfish Magazine.

I am indebted to my many wonderful teachers and mentors: Vahni Capildeo, Matthew Caley, Maura Dooley, Daljit Nagra, Blake Morrison, Nick Drake, Pascale Petit, Juliet Dusinberre, and Anne Fernihough. I am hugely grateful to Todd Swift, Rosanna Hildyard, and all at Eyewear Publishing, for making it happen.

Heartfelt thanks go also to my friends and colleagues who have supported me with feedback and beers over the years: Tom Bland, Alex Bell, David McGrath, Julia Rotte, Valeria Vescina, Bernadette Reed, Lynn Foote, Juliette Morton, Mark Grist, Richard Scott, Mark Walsh, Richard Gray, and all in my Poetry School classes, and Goldsmiths College groups. Thanks to all at The Vortex Jazz Club, especially Oliver Weindling, and to Girton College Cambridge University, Goldsmiths College University of London, and the Poetry School.

To my brilliant friends, all my thanks for everything.
And to my family, without whom this pamphlet would not exist: Jacqueline Ross, Bruno Heinen, Noemi Caruso, Ulrich Heinen, Elise Ross, Sacha Rattle, Zeynep Oszuca, Eliot Rattle, Elaine Heinen, Anna Heinen, and Benedict Heinen, thanks and love always.